DEDICATED TO MY MOTHER, ZAIRA Z. O'NEILL

False clownfish (*Amphiprion ocellaris*, 2 inches); Komodo National Park, Indonesia

WILD WATERS

PHOTO JOURNAL

MICHAEL PATRICK O'NEILL

BATFISH BOOKS

Assorted anthias species on the *Liberty* wreck; Tulamben, Bali

O'Neill, Michael Patrick
Wild Waters Photo Journal / Michael Patrick O'Neill
ISBN 978-0-9728653-6-4
Library of Congress Control Number: 2009909442

Printed in China

Batfish Books
PO Box 32909
Palm Beach Gardens, FL 33420-2909
www.batfishbooks.com

Photographer's Website:
www.mpostock.com

10 9 8 7 6 5 4 3 2 1

A diver explores Cannibal Rock in Komodo National Park, Indonesia

Photographer and goliath grouper (*Epinephelus itajara*, 7 ft.); Jupiter, FL

CONTENTS

FOREWORD

If you have the right eye, you can see that every place is special in its own way. Komodo is an exotic place. So is Florida. Exotic places are simply local for people living there. And the local is always the exotic for anyone from far away—or anyone who just hasn't looked.

Locals in spectacular or unique places often take their own backyard for granted. Places that ought to be cared for as the world's sacred trust have often been, and continue to be, hurt by people who either have no way of realizing that their place is unusual, or have no visible options. I'm not talking just about poor people in poor countries. The same often goes for Americans. We so easily fail to see the wild and special places in and around our own homes—or fail to defend them from destruction because we think it's someone else's job. Unfortunately for the lovelorn, "There are plenty of fish in the sea" is far less true today than it once was.

How to respond? First, to see. That's what this book is largely about. Once our eyes open, or while we spend our lives trying to better and better see, we may—and should let ourselves—fall in love. And then, what? We too often lose what we love because we let our love be passive. We must voice our love. We must defend our love with the realization that we are all part of one family of life. We must defend our family.

The task is vast, the stakes high. The first step: merely to see. And in seeing, to feel. Then, we must take others by the hand and help them see. This book is a set of prescription lenses for short-sightedness and fuzzy thinking. Michael Patrick O'Neill lends us his eyes, and by giving us a view to his heart, helps open ours.

Carl Safina

Carl Safina's books include Song for the Blue Ocean, Eye of the Albatross, *and* Voyage of the Turtle. *His writing has won the John Burroughs Medal for best nature book of the year; and the National Academies of Science, Medicine, and Engineering's Communication Award for the year's best book for communicating science. He is a MacArthur fellow and president of the Blue Ocean Institute.*

Great white shark (*Carcharodon carcharias*, 15 ft.); Guadalupe Island, Mexico

INTRODUCTION

Wild Waters is a pictorial and written journal illustrating a handful of vibrant and diverse aquatic ecosystems—Indonesia's Komodo National Park, Lembeh Strait and Bali; Brazil's Bonito region; Mexico's Guadalupe Island; and my home for the last twenty years, South Florida.

On a global scale, these locations cover insignificant, minute territory, but they are unique and contribute exponentially to our planet's richness. These hotspots of biological wealth deserve our immediate attention and care. At the very least, people should be aware of them to understand what's at stake when our actions threaten sensitive areas.

When I began this project two years ago, I purposely chose these places because they are where I like to photograph—the more remote and unknown, the better. Well, how about Bali and Florida? Believe me, they can still be rediscovered and photographed from an entirely new perspective. Fortunately, there's a lot of wild left in both, especially below the waterline.

I consider this to be my best work so far. *Wild Waters* showcases celebratory images as well as those depicting our heavy and messy footprints on the natural world. These photos are more relevant than ever because they can inspire us to make things better.

As you follow my bubbles in *Wild Waters*, I hope you enjoy my images as much as I enjoyed making them.

Michael Patrick O'Neill

American alligator (*Alligator mississippiensis*, 11 ft.); Big Cypress National Preserve, FL

KOMODO

Glassy sweepers (*Parapriacanthus ransonneti*, 2 inches)

CORAL REEF

Komodo's reefs are among the richest in the world. In the epicenter of the "Coral Triangle," a region encompassing Papua New Guinea, the Philippines, Solomon Islands, Indonesia and Malaysia, they shelter an all but incalculable assortment of species.

Home to more than 1,000 types of fish, 400 varieties of invertebrates, sea turtles and marine mammals, these reefs, part of Komodo National Park (overleaf), are a marine biologist's paradise.

"One of the most exciting aspects of diving and photographing in Komodo is the chance to encounter marine animals still unknown to science.

"During a frigid night dive in Horseshoe Bay, I stumbled upon two such animals: a type of dragon moray (10 inches, top) and a torpedo ray (9 inches, right), which, if provoked, reportedly can discharge an electric shock of 200 volts. To date, Horseshoe Bay is the only location where this strange ray is found."

A hawksbill sea turtle (*Eretmochelys imbricata*, 3 ft.) visits Cannibal Rock looking for sponges.

KINGDOM OF THE CRINOIDS

In a spectacular show of color, crinoids paint Cannibal Rock from top to bottom. These plankton feeders, related to starfish and part of the *Crinoidea* family, make this site a favorite of SCUBA divers.

Located in the southern end of the park, this area was named by pioneering divers after they observed a Komodo dragon preying on a smaller conspecific on a nearby hill.

A guide describes how the Komodo dragon ambushes its prey.

KOMODO DRAGON (*VARANUS KOMODOENSIS*, 9 FT.)

Earth's remaining Komodo dragons reside within the park. These massive monitor lizards rely on their extraordinary sense of smell, speed, sharp teeth, claws and venomous saliva to hunt down and kill pigs, deer and even buffalo.

Habitat destruction and the elimination of prey species by poachers pose the biggest threats to these legendary creatures, of which only 2,000 remain.

CLARK'S ANEMONE FISH WITH EGGS (AMPHIPRION CLARKII, 5 INCHES)

A dedicated parent, a female Clark's anemone fish aerates her eggs with rapid movements of her tail and fins. The tiny embryos, clearly visible, will soon hatch and dissipate in the water column. They enter their watery world on the very bottom of the food chain, with predators eating the overwhelming majority.

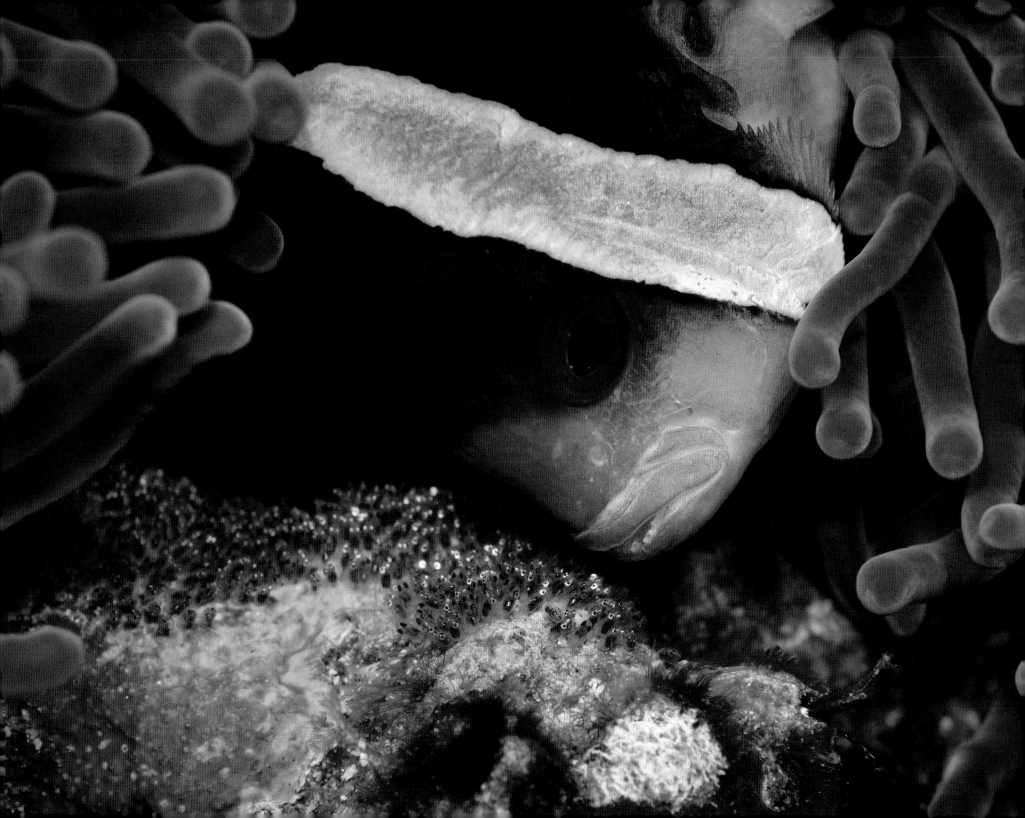

CHECKERBOARD WRASSE (*HALICHOERES HORTULANUS*, 8 INCHES)

This stunning fish is just one example of hermaphroditism in the marine environment.

Hermaphroditic animals can be both male and female concurrently or sequentially. In this case, this fish is protogynous—it started life as a female and later turned into a male, or more specifically, a super male.

As a super male, he guards a harem of females in a territory he controls. From a biological standpoint, there's a big advantage to being the super male. The ability to breed with many females gives him a greater chance of passing on his genes to future generations.

When he dies, the next largest fish of the same species replaces him. This replacement may be another male, or a female from his own harem that changes into a male.

"I set out to do a late afternoon dive to observe the reef at dusk, a magical moment when the 'midnight shift' replaces diurnal animals.

"Like a city during rush hour, this habitat at nightfall is a blur of motion, with fish hurrying for cover. As he swam past, I panned the camera and pressed the shutter."

*"One of the highlights of my latest Komodo trip included diving near sandy areas and photographing two favorites, the yellow-barred jawfish (*Opistognathus *sp., 7 inches, top) and the white margin stargazer (*Uranoscopus sulphureus, *17 inches, opposite).*

"The male jawfish incubates his mate's fertilized eggs in his mouth for about one week before releasing the miniscule fry. It took me nearly two days of searching to find a mouthbrooding male and then to photograph him.

"Named for its skyward stare, the stargazer will never win any beauty pageant, but what this bogeyman of the depths lacks in looks, it more than makes up in fascinating behavior.

"Notice how this specimen uses its ribbon-like tongue to lure unsuspecting fish near its cavernous mouth."

One of the biggest threats facing Komodo is the steady influx of people who tax its abundant natural resources.

These settlers, whose numbers have ballooned since 1950, established villages inside the park. They polluted waterways and threatened both terrestrial and marine animals.

Fishermen in particular have caused tremendous damage to the ecosystem by adopting unsustainable fishing practices.

"One hot afternoon, I swam over to these men who were getting ready to pluck giant clams from the reef. Destitute, all they had were the bare essentials for the job: Styrofoam blocks and paddles to move around and rudimentary fins and masks.

"Nearby, one of their colleagues proudly displayed a prized game fish, a giant trevally (Caranx ignobilis), caught jigging near the coral.

"While the reefs and their inhabitants are officially protected, enforcement of environmental laws is sporadic."

"Using homemade, fertilizer-based explosives, 'reef bombers' in Komodo once destroyed many pristine reefs to catch as much fish as possible—and demolished everything else in the process. In a matter of seconds, they transformed cathedrals of coral into mounds of lifeless rubble.

"They targeted not only small fish, like the schooling fusiliers in the photo, but predators as well. An initial blast first obliterated the fusiliers. Then, when giant trevallies, groupers and snappers moved in to feast on the dead fish, the fishermen detonated a secondary, more powerful bomb embedded deep in the reef, killing the incoming big fish.

"Once the underwater terrain was leveled and the fish were cleaned, salted and dried in the sun, the bombers moved on to the next reef.

"This went on until the mid-1990s, when conservationists and police patrols successfully battled the fishermen. After arrests and even gunfights, the bombers were eventually driven out. A determined lot, however, they didn't go far. Today, they continue to operate with impunity just outside the park's boundary.

"This became abundantly clear when a loud underwater explosion rocked our group during a dive at Sangean, a volcanic island beyond the protected zone. It completely shattered any illusions I might have had that blast fishing was a thing of the past.

"Komodo's reefs are now silent, and I hope that nature's powers continue to heal the ugly wounds without any further setbacks."

LEMBEH

Spiny Devilfish (*Inimicus didactylus*, 6 inches)

At first glance, the floor of the channel separating Lembeh Island (above) from Sulawesi in Indonesia appears lifeless and empty. Black volcanic sand and rotting vegetation cover the entire seabed. The only landmarks in this featureless, monochromatic realm are the odd coral head, rusty can or discarded net.

Yet, this unsightly place is home to a rich community filled with the sea's most bizarre creatures, all suited to thrive in this wasteland below the waves.

Let's take a look at what might be swimming, crawling and lurking in this fabled and gritty underworld.

Mimicking the poisonous banded sea krait, a saddled eel (*Myrichthys colubrinus*, 24 inches) tricks its enemies and forages unafraid in the open.

Fake eyes cover the entire body of the juvenile polka-dot grouper (*Cromileptes altivelis*, 7 inches). Known as eyespots, these black markings confuse predators and help prevent a fatal strike to the head.

The yellow shrimp goby (*Cryptocentrus cinctus*, 3 inches) is just one of many goby species found i

ADDLE-FLAP SCORPIONFISH (*RHINOPIAS ESCHMEYERI*, 6 INCHES)

med for its peculiar fins, the paddle-flap scorpionfish is a bottom-dwelling, venomous fish
und only in a handful of locations in the Indo-Pacific.

elies on its impeccable camouflage for protection and hunting. Incidentally, it stands out in
ese photos because of the underwater flashes, which illuminate colors that otherwise would
absorbed by the murky water.

so known by its genus name, *Rhinopias*, it's easily identifiable. Like the other 5 to 10
embers of the family, it has an upturned nose, compressed body and eyes positioned at the
o of the head.

vers travel to the most distant corners of Asia for a chance encounter with this master
nter, and Lembeh has become the favorite spot to find it.

BANGGAI CARDINALFISH (*PTERAPOGON KAUDERNI*, 3 INCHES)

Aquarists all over the world covet the Banggai cardinalfish for its striking color, shape and pattern. Demand for it is so great that it's now endangered in the wild.

To make matters worse, its small population and extremely limited range make it a prime candidate for extinction. A natural disaster or a man-made accident, like an oil spill, could potentially exterminate it.

In 2000, tropical fish collectors released Banggai cardinalfish into Lembeh Strait, 250 miles from its original home. The species is now well established there, but the impact of this introduction on the native fish remains to be seen.

This gorgeous animal is a paternal mouthbrooder. Males incubate the eggs and young in their mouths for 30 days while protected by the females. This parental care gives the brood a much greater chance of surviving than if it were on its own.

Like a coral snake, a white-spotted nudibranch (*Chromodoris albopunctata*, 6 inches) uses its intense colors to warn foes of its toxicity. This marine cousin of the snail is carnivorous and feeds on anemones and corals.

Poisonous compounds found in the muscles of the flamboyant cuttlefish (*Metasepia pfefferi*, 2 inches) are as deadly as those from a close relative and fellow mollusk, the blue ring octopus.

NIGHT DIVE

After sundown, nocturnal animals awaken to patrol the underwater plains of Lembeh Strait.

An anemone hermit crab (*Dardanus pedunculatus*, 4 inches, top) feels its way through the volcanic sand looking for decaying matter and discarded bait from fishermen. Named for the anemones that decorate and protect its shell, this crustacean is an essential member of the ocean's clean-up crew.

The size of a grape, the bobtail squid (*Euphrymna berryi*, 1 inch, left) has forged a special relationship with bioluminescent bacteria that enables it to hunt in the dark. Located in the squid's light organ, a chamber near the underbelly, the glowing bacteria help keep the cephalopod concealed while it pursues small fish and shrimp.

"Discarded by people on boats and coastal communities, garbage makes its way to the farthest corners of the sea, where it remains unseen by most. Metals, plastics and fishing nets can take hundreds of years to break down.

"Often, the debris that accumulates on the bottom serves as a suitable base for soft and hard corals to colonize. Polyps of these species settle on these mountains of trash and grow, eventually covering the entire structure. Fish and other sea life soon follow.

"Will the coral reefs of the future look like this?"

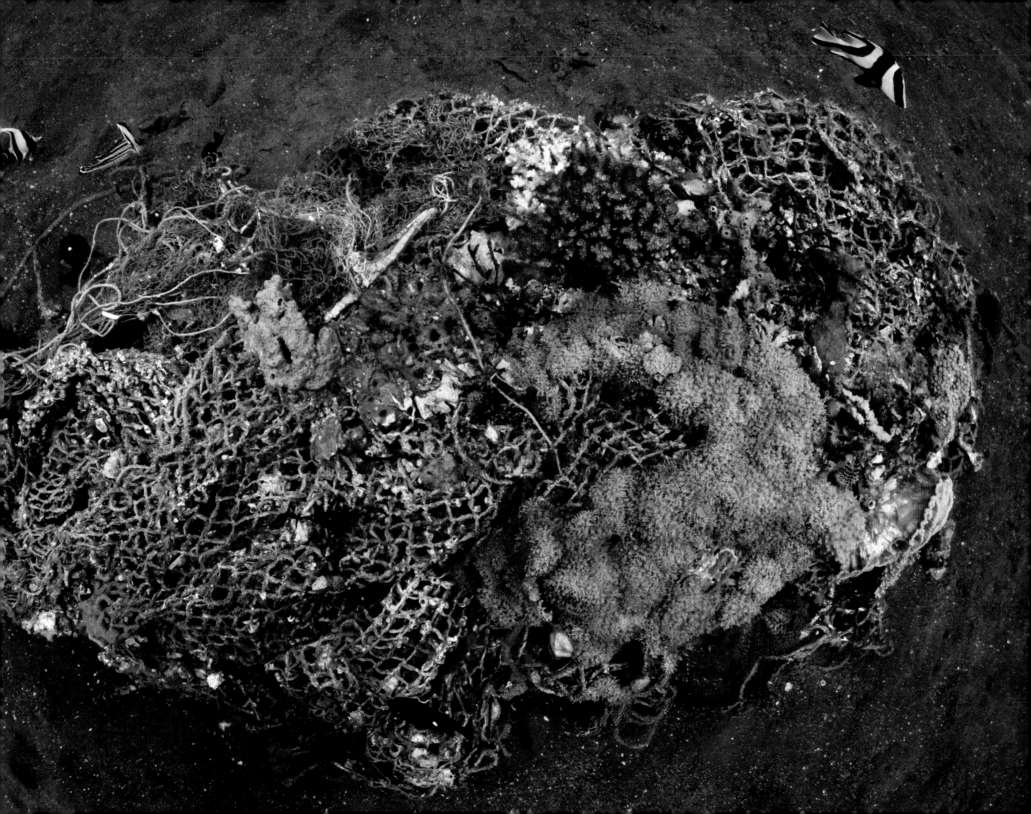

BALI

"Prior to diving at Tulamben on Bali's northeast coast, I visited a busy fish market to see what the Javanese fishermen were selling after hoisting their boats on the beach (previous spread).

"The stalls overflowed with marine life, testament to the island's prolific waters. Sardines (bottom left), crabs wrapped in leaves (bottom right), and colorful parrotfish (opposite), among other species, were sold quickly after being unloaded."

"THE DIVING HELPER CLUB"

Established in 1978 and made up of women, "The Diving Helper Club" carries SCUBA equipment for tourists diving along Tulamben's rocky beaches. The nominal fee charged by the porters helps generate extra income for this remote fishing village.

The area's biggest draw is the fantastic wreck of the *Liberty* (right), a World War II cargo ship torpedoed by the Japanese in 1942. The 395 ft. vessel is so encrusted with corals and invertebrates that it barely resembles a man-made structure.

The *Liberty* is a treasure chest of living jewels. Portrayed clockwise from the left: orange-lined triggerfish (*Balistapus undulatus*, 9 inches), white-lined grouper (*Anyperodon leucogrammicus*, 12 inches) and coral grouper (*Cephalopholis miniata*, 10 inches).

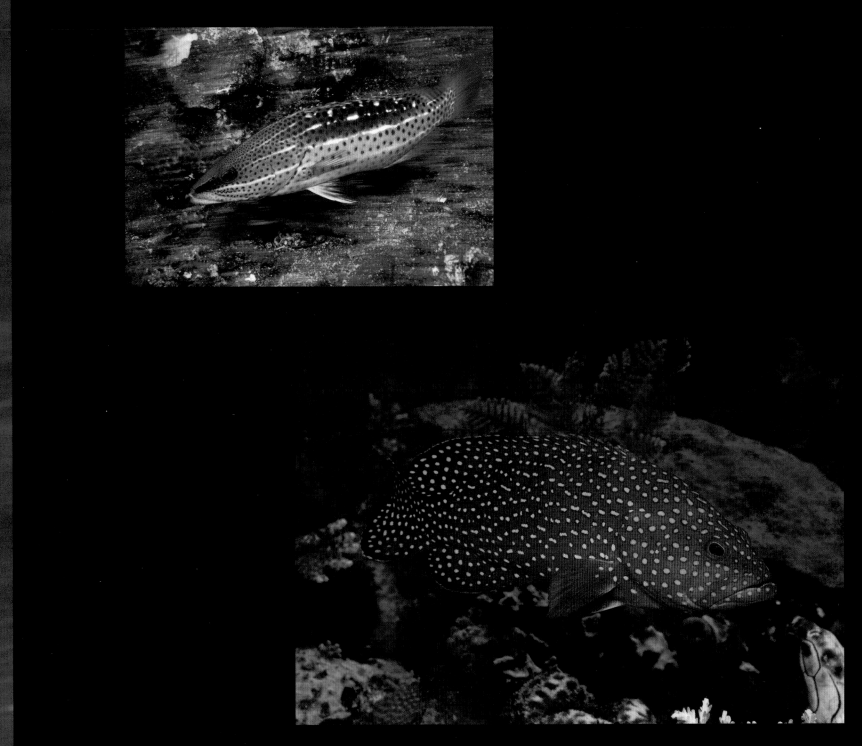

EMPEROR ANGELFISH (*POMACANTHUS IMPERATOR*, 16 INCHES)

The most regal of all angelfish, the emperor undergoes a dramatic color change from the juvenile stage (below) to its adult form (left).

The aquarium trade avidly targets this species with consumers paying up to $250 for a single fish. If only they knew the destructive toll the trade takes on the environment and fishermen, they would not buy the majority of Indo-Pacific saltwater fish available for sale.

The fishermen rely on faulty dive gear, lack safety training and, for the most part, use potassium cyanide to stun (and poison) the fish, reef and possibly themselves. Unfortunately, most fish die en route to the retailer. Collectors earn very little money, while middlemen make the lion's share.

While found on the *Liberty*, the emperor is more readily observed on tiny reefs and other man-made structures along Tulamben's volcanic ocean bottom.

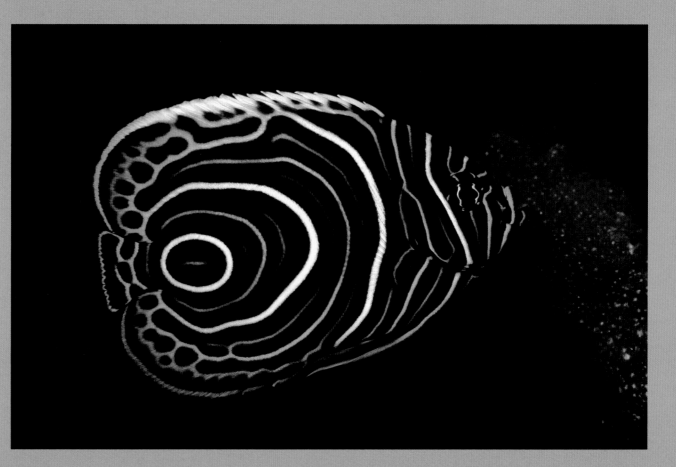

"Natural and artificial habitats, like this coral patch (left) and metal dome (above), are oases of life in an otherwise drab underwater landscape. These structures, about the size of the average living room carpet, are home to hundreds of animals.

"I routinely spent up to four hours per day photographing these ecosystems. Without exception, I ran out of air before running out of subjects to examine and photograph."

"The lowly shrimp, thought of only as food by people, plays many roles in a tropical sea. What consumed so much of my time in Tulamben was capturing images of these crustaceans living and working in their Lilliputian universes.

"With a home few would desire, a pair of Coleman shrimp (Periclimenes colemani, 2 inches, left) lives happily protected among the iridescent spines of a fire urchin (Asthenosoma varium, 12 inches).

"A white-striped cleaner shrimp (Lysmata amboinensis, 3 inches, top left) has little to fear from this juvenile giant moray (Gymnothorax javanicus, 2 ft.). It mans a cleaning station, a spot on the reef that can be thought of as an underwater carwash. There, it removes parasites, scales and dead skin from the bigger fish.

"The blotchy shrimp goby (Amblyeleotris periophthalma, 4 inches) and alpheid shrimp (Alpheus sp., 2 inches, top right) share the same home. Possessing excellent vision, the fish remains on the doorstep of the tunnel, looking out for danger. The shrimp, on the other hand, constantly expands and repairs their subterranean abode. They continually touch each other. Whenever the goby feels threatened, it dives into the hole, with the shrimp following immediately behind."

GUADALUPE

GUADALUPE ISLAND, MEXICO

Since 2000, Guadalupe Island in the Eastern Pacific has been the preferred location for observing the great white shark. Its transparent waters, proximity to the United States and reliable shark population helped it trump hotspots like South Africa and Australia. Situated 230 miles from Ensenada, Mexico, this Manhattan-sized island is bone dry, with rocky cliffs and little vegetation.

The sharks are seasonal visitors, arriving in August and departing in December. The smaller males show up first, followed by much larger females. The abundance of marine mammals is one of the reasons they prowl the waters of this remote island.

Targeted prey includes the northern elephant seal (*Mirounga angustirostris*, 14 ft., top), California sea lion (*Zalophus californianus*, 8 ft., right) and Guadalupe fur seal (*Arctocephalus townsendi*, 7 ft., opposite). While they can satisfy a great white's appetite, they are not easy to catch. These animals are

"It's a commitment to photograph great whites in Guadalupe. Since there are no facilities, visitors travel to the island on extended range vessels and remain on them for the whole week. Every expedition is different. Some are exceptional, while others are a total failure.

"They are also expensive. Any trip that includes boats, fuel, remote locations and sharks (especially great whites) carries a heavy price tag. Despite a disappointing trip to South Africa a few years earlier, I decided to try my luck again. Thankfully, the outcome of this one was worth every penny.

"Following the 24-hour crossing from Mexico, the crew lowers the cages into the water, and after that, the baiting and waiting begins."

GREAT WHITE SHARK (CARCHARODON CARCHARIAS, 15 FT.)

The great white, the largest predatory fish, belongs to the Mackerel family of sharks, which includes the mako, sand tiger and thresher. It ranges primarily offshore South Africa, South Australia, New England and California because these inhospitable waters harbor its well-insulated, blubbery prey.

Although great whites occasionally bite people, experts prefer to call these rare encounters accidents rather than attacks. In most cases, the sharks mistake swimmers and surfers for their natural food. Luckily, most realize they have made an error and release their victims, who almost always survive.

Scientists recently discovered that great whites travel enormous distances. In 2004, South African researchers equipped a young female with a satellite-tracking transmitter to follow her movements along the coast. They were surprised to learn that the shark, named Nicole, completed a 12,000 mile journey from South Africa to Australia and back in only nine months. They believe she found her way using the earth's magnetic field or possibly the position of the sun, stars and moon.

Nicole's adventure demonstrates the global range of these endangered fish and the need to create protected corridors in the oceans where migratory animals travel.

"As it approaches, this 15 ft. great white seems happy to see me. Without a doubt, it would really be smiling if I weren't in the cage.

"This species is the only one an experienced diver shouldn't photograph outside the cage. It's so powerful, cunning and unpredictable that, in my opinion, the risks are far too great.

"Experts often say this charismatic monster acts like a ghost of the depths. Like a cat, it's sneaky and almost imperceptible. Even in Guadalupe's clear waters, it's able to creep up right next to the cage and give you the scare of your life."

"Our insatiable passion for everything great white is matched only by the beast's legendary appetite.

"People, especially children, just can't seem to get enough—from movies, books, magazines and television. A teacher once told me that for kids, 'It's all about sharks and dinosaurs.' I believe her.

"Giant dinosaurs are not around anymore, but how long will sharks be? Will our favorite fish vanish in the near future? Unfortunately, that could happen in our lifetime.

"On a worldwide basis, unsustainable fishing has already reduced many shark populations by 90%. The situation is critical. The general public is not alarmed simply because this environmental crime is occurring in the high seas, unseen except by the perpetrators. Demand for shark fins (to make soup) is driving the slaughter globally.

"There are also the issues of poaching and trafficking, especially with great whites. According to the National Oceanic and Atmospheric Administration (NOAA) Office of Law Enforcement, the jaws of a great white can sell anywhere from $8,000 to $22,000.

"These sharks are officially protected in the United States, Mexico, Australia, South Africa and a handful of other countries, but the enforcement of laws is difficult. Teeth and jaws are sold openly in retail establishments and on the Internet."

BONITO

Brazilian law mandates that property owners in Bonito keep the shoreline of rivers, such as the Rio Sucuri, wooded to prevent erosion.

A local aquatic plant (*Echinodorus macrophyllus*) has been targeted for study because of its medicinal properties. It's a natural diuretic and helps treat rheumatic diseases.

"I was floored the first time I saw a documentary on Bonito's exceptionally clear streams. It seemed as if the fish and plants floated on air, and that divers swam in the largest, cleanest aquarium on the planet.

"After quite a bit of research, I decided it warranted a visit. Even though Bonito, located in the state of Mato Grosso do Sul in southwestern Brazil, is far removed from the ocean, it offered an entirely new underwater environment to explore and photograph.

"I was born and raised in Brazil and always wanted to return there to photograph. Looking back, I consider this my favorite trip."

Water erupts from a spring in the Rio da Prata.

Prehistoric seas once covered Bonito, and bygone coral reefs deposited abundant reserves of limestone. A porous rock that removes impurities from water, limestone filters the underground aquifer, making local rivers some of the clearest anywhere.

While Bonito is well known in Brazil, it remains largely undiscovered by outsiders. One of its attractions is its incomparable fluvial habitat—a peculiarity in a country known for its huge, muddy rivers like the Amazon.

In full display are freshwater fish and jungle animals that otherwise would be hidden from view in the sediment-rich rivers.

Bonito sits atop a labyrinth of more than 100 caves. Here, 230 ft. underground, cavers explore the Grotto of the Blue Lagoon.

CUVIER'S DWARF CAIMAN (*PALEOSUCHUS PALPEBROSUS*, 5 FT.)

Resting on the bottom of the Rio da Prata, a female Cuvier's dwarf caiman poses no threat to visitors who enjoy the crystalline spring on a daily basis. One of the smallest crocodilians, it lives on fish and crustaceans.

Scientists believe its extra thick skin is an adaptation to protect it from large predators and rocks in fast flowing jungle rivers. The tough hide has also served this reptile well in an entirely different way—poachers never targeted the species when other caimans were killed by the millions in Brazil in the 1980s to supply the luxury leather trade.

"I knew my trip to Bonito was going to be great when I encountered this caiman on the very first day of shooting. It's rare to have this kind of opportunity right in the beginning of the expedition—in my case, within two hours of arriving at the spring. Typically, you have to pay your dues, since wild animals don't take appointments.

"This spectacular caiman kept her babies hidden in the dense vegetation near the water's edge while she rested motionless on the river bottom.

"I walked slowly to keep the water around her clear and stayed as far away as possible from her hatchlings. I was using a fisheye lens, and in order to fill the frame and take compelling photos, I had to get close, very close.

"Unlike the American alligator, this species is not very aggressive, so getting near was fine as long as she had an escape route. I started taking pictures from 4 ft. away, coming up for air after every 5 or 6 shots. I finally crawled to a mere 8 inches from her. My heart pounded!"

GREEN ANACONDA (*EUNECTES MURINUS*, 16 FT.)

At home underwater in a thicket of branches, a green anaconda explores the Rio Formoso. This giant snake, found in South America's tropical wetlands, is the largest in the Western Hemisphere and second in size only to the reticulated python from Southeast Asia. The female, the larger of the sexes, can weigh 400 lbs. and preys on caiman, capybaras, birds, fish and turtles. While any animal weighing up to 100 lbs. is fair game, there are no credible reports of green anacondas eating people.

It hunts silently and patiently, usually at the water's edge. Once its target is within range, it strikes with blinding speed. Suitably, *Sucuri*, the snake's name in Tupi-Guarani, a native Brazilian dialect, means "the one that bites quickly." A constrictor, the green anaconda subdues its quarry by squeezing until all breathing stops.

"My goal in Bonito was to photograph a green anaconda underwater. One day, my guide heard that a large snake was sunning herself every afternoon on a remote jungle river, so we decided to go there the next day and take a look. At first, I dismissed the reported dimensions of the snake as pure exaggeration, but when we finally saw her, I realized the locals weren't joking. Coiled, she was the size of a bathtub.

"It was a late afternoon in June, almost wintertime, and we—snake included—were in for a chilly night. A shadow finally covered her bed, and the queen of the river slid into the water.

"Very reluctantly, I followed. The rocks hurt my bare feet as I walked around chest-deep, trying to find the 16 ft. snake in the branches. This was insane. I started to shiver and realized something was watching me.

"There! She rested on a submerged branch, and her olive and brown skin made her practically invisible in the fading light. I started shooting and leaned closer. In response, she stretched out towards me, completely unafraid. In between shots, I admired this brute—her cloudy eyes, immense girth and weathered hide.

"Without warning, she moved, and I jumped out of the way. The snake vanished, leaving me breathless."

Protected from fishing, Bonito's rivers shelter healthy fish stocks. The dourado (*Salminus brasiliensis*, 4 ft., top) is the largest predatory fish in the springs. Coveted for its tasty flesh and fighting spirit, it has been overfished in many parts of its range in south-central Brazil. Opposite, tiny jewels abound near vegetation: an unidentified tetra (*Moenkhausia* sp., 2 inches, top right) and a favorite of aquarists, the serpae tetra (*Hyphessobrycon eques*, 2 inches, bottom right), found in abundance.

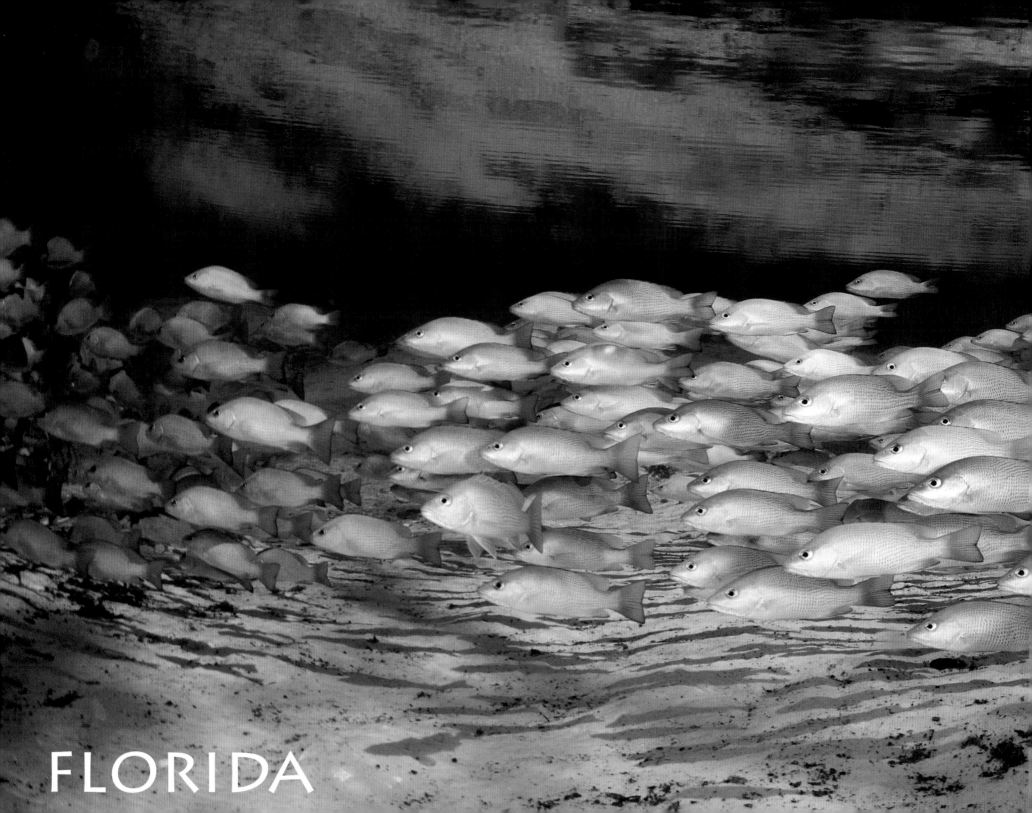

FLORIDA

Grey snappers (*Lutjanus griseus*, 10 inches); Crystal River, FL

CORAL REEF, JUNO BEACH

Despite the state's burgeoning population, Florida possesses vast marine habitats and resources. The reefs along its southeast coast contribute $6 billion in revenue annually to the economy and generate 60,000 jobs in the fishing, diving and boating industries.

They are far richer than the majority of reefs in the Caribbean, most of which have been depleted. Those in northern Palm Beach County arguably offer the best diving in the country.

These rocky reefs, heavily encrusted with colorful sponges (left), harbor a staggering collection of animals, many rare and hard to find.

Batwing crab (*Carpilius corallinus*, 6 inches); Palm Beach, FL

LEATHERBACK SEA TURTLE (*DERMOCHELYS CORIACEA*, 9 FT.), JUPITER

In a class entirely of its own, the leatherback sea turtle is one of the largest reptiles, reaching more than 1,500 lbs. in weight. Shaped like a giant hydrodynamic teardrop, it can dive to over 4,000 ft.—deeper than most whales—thanks to a flexible shell that compresses as the water pressure increases.

Global trekkers, these creatures travel enormous distances. The population that nests in Southeast Florida goes to northern Canada to feed, and Indonesian leatherbacks forage in Monterey Bay, California. They complete these incredible journeys on a diet of just jellyfish.

While this present-day dinosaur has survived cataclysmic changes for over 100 million years, it's having difficulty coexisting with modern man. Poaching, egg collecting and habitat degradation all take a heavy toll. Furthermore, thousands die trapped in fishing equipment. Populations in the Pacific are in dire straits, while those in the Atlantic appear stable and perhaps are even increasing.

"With outstretched wings spanning 8 ft., this male leatherback approached so close that his flipper brushed my arm. He shot upward and made a barrel roll, all the while staring at me. Then, satisfied I posed no threat, the colossus glided into the murk.

"Ever since photographing my first one, eight years earlier, I had dreamt of a repeat but never imagined it would happen this way. I chartered a boat and went to a spot where fishermen were seeing the giants. It was late in the season and time was running out.

"This remote reef is where commercial spearfishermen hunt groupers and snappers for restaurants. Aggressive sharks often approach during the decompression stop, making the dives harrowing and intense. The site—stomping grounds for the world's most glorious reptile—can leave you breathless and with strong palpitations.

"However, an image of an incoming leatherback in its element—the open ocean—is one of the holy grails of wildlife photography. By the end of this special day, I had seen four different turtles and photographed two of them."

LOGGERHEAD SEA TURTLE (*CARETTA CARETTA*, 4 FT.), PALM BEACH COUNTY

Divers and beachgoers encounter loggerhead sea turtles most often during the summer, when the 300 lb. reptiles mate (right) and come ashore to nest.

Regularly seen in Florida—home to half of the world's loggerhead population—they are highly endangered elsewhere. In Baja California alone, 2,000 drown every year in nets.

Giving a helping hand, volunteers and staff of the Loggerhead Marinelife Center of Juno Beach prepare to release a turtle after rehabilitation (top). The center plays a vital role nursing injured turtles back to health and promoting marine conservation.

WHALE SHARK (*RHINCODON TYPUS*, 30 FT.), PALM BEACH

The largest fish on Earth dwarfs snorkelers during a late fall dive trip. Highly migratory, whale sharks pass through the area in cooler months following plankton and small fish.

The International Union for Conservation of Nature (IUCN) has categorized the whale shark as "vulnerable to extinction" in its Red List database, a worldwide reference of endangered wildlife.

The gentle giants are under assault in the Far East, where they are hunted for their fins and flesh.

CREATURES OF THE SAND, SINGER ISLAND

The estuary near the Palm Beach Inlet is known for its bizarre and uncommon animals. Living underneath bridges, around litter, and even buried in the sand, this hardy bunch tolerates extreme variations in water pollution, salinity and temperature with the ebb and flow of the tides.

The seldom seen bandtail sea robin (*Prionotus ophryas*, 8 inches, top) relies on finger-like pectoral fins to sift for food—small shrimp and fish—hidden in the gravel.

The lined seahorse (*Hippocampus erectus*, 6 inches, right), can be found with its tail wrapped around sponges near bridge pilings. This delicate and shy species is a poor swimmer and a challenge to find, for both divers and predators.

The northern stargazer (*Astroscopus guttatus*, 22 inches, opposite) uses its pectoral fins to bury itself in the muck. Unlike most fish, it breathes through its nostrils and can discharge an electric shock if threatened. Fleshy appendages, resembling an oversized zipper, prevent sand from entering its mouth.

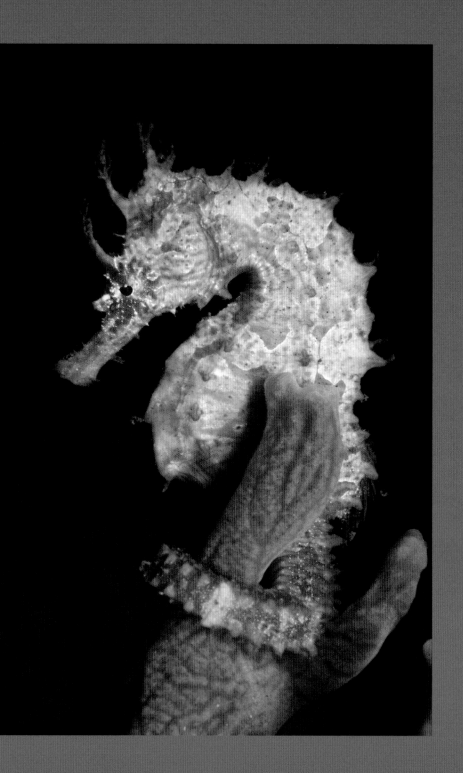

IMPERILED REEFS

Reckless human activity jeopardizes the long-term viability of local reefs and their inhabitants.

Clockwise from the right: remains of a loggerhead sea turtle killed by a boater in northern Palm Beach County; reef contaminated by bleach used to catch lobsters for human consumption in Juno; beach renourishment program at Singer Island that suffocates inshore reefs with excess sand; and bundles of rope litter the ocean floor offshore Palm Beach.

Anhinga Trail, Everglades National Park (top); Peninsula cooter hatchling (*Pseudemys floridana peninsularis,* 1 inch, opposite); Big Cypress National Preserve

EVERGLADES NATIONAL PARK

Designated in 1979 by the United Nations Educational, Scientific and Cultural Organization (UNESCO) as a location of special value to mankind, the Florida Everglades is the only subtropical wetland in the United States.

Even though most people think of it as a swamp, it's actually a river that flows at a rate of a quarter mile every 24 hours. Extending from Lake Okeechobee to Florida Bay in the southern portion of the state, this 4,300 square mile ecosystem is shaped by drought, fire, water and extreme weather. Its forests, grassy plains, canals and brackish estuaries are rich in wildlife.

While a patchwork of preserves and parks protects large sections of this unique and cherished region, development and agriculture continue to chip away tiny bits of it every year. Other threats include pollution, flood control and the introduction of exotic plant and animal species. State and Federal officials have pledged to restore this treasured environment in a massive, long-term project. Only time will tell if they can succeed.

ALLIGATOR (*ALLIGATOR MISSISSIPPIENSIS*, 8 FT.), FAKAHATCHEE STRAND

The American alligator, symbol of the Everglades, is a conservation success story.

Nearly eradicated in the early 20th century, it has made a remarkable recovery. In fact, it's safe to assume that where there is fresh water in the Sunshine State, there are alligators.

These ancient lizards possess one of the strongest bites in the animal kingdom. Lined with 74 to 80 teeth, their jaws apply astonishing pressure.

Opportunistic carnivores, they eat a wide range of creatures—from fish and frogs to freshwater turtles and deer. They often attack pets and can become extremely dangerous, especially if fed by people.

Females are dedicated parents. This one is guarding her nest, a mound visible in the background. She remains close to it for 65 days and readily attacks any intruder that threatens the safety of her 35 to 50 eggs incubating beneath layers of warm dirt and rotting vegetation.

When the hatchlings emerge from the nest in late summer, they will remain with her for up to two years. Despite her extraordinary care, raccoons, birds, bobcats and fish will eat the majority of the babies.

A young manatee plays with a tourist in Three Sisters Spring, Crystal River, FL.

MANATEE (*TRICHECHUS MANATUS LATIROSTRIS*, 12 FT.), CRYSTAL RIVER

The charismatic Florida manatee, or sea cow, can easily assume the role of protagonist in a story that describes the negative impact of human activity on Florida's environment. Practically everything we do along the state's coastline impacts it—unfortunately, in a detrimental way. It is threatened by pollution, red tides, habitat loss and the boating industry. Only 3,000 are left in the wild.

There are three species: West Indian (which includes the Florida subspecies), West African and Amazonian. All are endangered, distant relatives of the elephant and originated from a land-based ancestor 60 million years ago. They, along with the dugong, a related species from Asia, are the only marine mammals to be completely herbivorous.

Manatees spend countless hours eating underwater vegetation and consume up to 10% of their body weight in plants every day. They weigh up to 1,200 lbs., with females being larger than males.

CRYSTAL RIVER

Crystal River is the hub for manatee encounters. Situated in Florida's northwest corner, the town was named for its traditionally clear springs. Lamentably, most are now turbid after years of development.

Highly sensitive to cold weather, manatees leave the chilly Gulf of Mexico in November and enter the town's springs, which remain a constant 72° F. There, they comfortably ride out frequent cold fronts that drop the air temperature well below freezing.

By late March, they return to the Gulf and scatter along the coastline.

EPILOGUE

"On the last day of shooting for Wild Waters *in Bali, I was given a special opportunity.*

"A twilight breeze along Tulamben's rocky beach enticed a young boy to play with his miniature jukung. The handmade replica of the traditional Balinese fishing boat even had a working sail made from a plastic bag and was held together only by string.

"Standing in the surf, the boy pushed the tiny boat into deeper water. A gust took over where he left off, filling the fragile sail and carrying the model out to sea. He worked a nearly invisible fishing line, his only connection to his prized possession, and the jukung came to life, maneuvering just like the real thing. He reeled it in and repeated the process over and over. This ritual continued until the golden light vanished.

"He left, and I returned to the little resort where I was staying. I knew then that I would use this photo to conclude Wild Waters, *a project that consumed over two years. It gave me unforgettable, life-changing moments, not only with amazing animals but, more importantly, with people from all walks of life who, like me, are mesmerized by the ocean."*